LIVE Video Revolution

"If live video is on your radar at all, and you want to improve your skills and become a true live streaming champion. Then I highly recommend that you enroll in The Live Video Academy."

— **Owen Hemsath**, Video Marketing Coach

"If you have not read this man's book, you need to consume the content that he puts out, because it is simply top-notch. Anything on live video marketing I study and implement because it works."

— **John Lee Dumas**, Host of Entrepreneur on Fire Podcast

LIVE Video Revolution

**How to Get Massive Customer Engagement
and Skyrocket Sales with Live Video**

joel comm

NEW YORK

NASHVILLE • MELBOURNE • VANCOUVER

LIVE Video Revolution
How to Get Massive Customer Engagement and Skyrocket Sales with Live Video

Published in New York, New York, by Morgan James Publishing. Morgan James is a trademark of Morgan James, LLC. www.MorganJamesPublishing.com

The Morgan James Speakers Group can bring authors to your live event. For more information or to book an event visit The Morgan James Speakers Group at www.TheMorganJamesSpeakersGroup.com.

Cover Design: Matt Clark / ImageDesigns.com

ISBN 978-1-68350-613-3 paperback
ISBN 978-1-68350-614-0 eBook
Library of Congress Control Number: 2017908933

In an effort to support local communities, raise awareness and funds, Morgan James Publishing donates a percentage of all book sales for the life of each book to Habitat for Humanity Peninsula and Greater Williamsburg.

Get involved today! Visit
www.MorganJamesBuilds.com

Table of Contents

Foreword

"Let's see if this thing works," I thought to myself.

I pulled out my phone, opened Facebook, and typed the words "testing Facebook Live."

I smiled and pushed the button.

In mere seconds something happened that—for the first time in my life—left me speechless.

A few months earlier, I witnessed a few people slowly walking around trade shows with their eyes glued to their outstretched hands.

Without fail, they knew what they were holding was the beginning of something big.

And the people watching from laptops and phones around the planet were fascinated.

So when I went live for the first time, I had some idea what might happen. But I was still shocked.

In the first few seconds there were 70 people watching me live.

Then it jumped to 300...

Within 10 seconds more than 1,000 people were watching live!

All at once I thought "what the heck," "wow, this is crazy," "oh, the possibilities," and "wait, there's a 1,000 people here!!"

Nothing could have prepared me for that moment. The paradigm just shifted into high gear.

Joel Comm was right.

Live video was a new way to connect with people, raw and unedited.

I gathered the team at Social Media Examiner. We mapped out a plan to start a weekly live show and add a live video track to our conference.

I started talking about this new medium on my podcast and frankly everywhere. I just wanted to help people understand the opportunity live video presented.

Have you caught the bug yet?

Do you know what live video can do for you?

Live video is the true manifestation of social media. It's the next best thing to being in-person with a group of your biggest fans.

It allows you to educate, inform, entertain, and sell!

And it does it in the most authentic way possible because it's live. There are no do-overs. People accept you as you are, mistakes and all.

It's precisely because it's imperfect that people love it.

Joel is a torchbearer for the live video revolution. Read this book and just jump in.

You'll never know what doors it unlocks for you unless you try.

And just maybe, you'll be more prepared than I was.

– **Michael A. Stelzner**, Founder, Social Media Examiner and Social Media Marketing World.

Academy.live

Preface

The year was 2016.

Candace Payne, a housewife from Grand Prairie, Texas had just left her local Kohl's Department store with a new purchase in her hand. Stepping into her vehicle, the excitement of what she bought turned into a desire to go live on her Facebook page so she could see the newly acquired item with her friends that might tune in to watch.

This was no professional production. The set was Candace's vehicle. There wasn't time to get hair and makeup on point. There was no script. There was no director.

She pushed the live button Facebook, but she could never have seen what would happen next.

160 million views later, the world is now very familiar with "Chewbacca Mom," the name affectionately given to Candace when her unveiling and wearing of the Star Wars Chewbacca mask that made the trademark growl when the mouth opened was foisted on an unsuspecting public.

But it wasn't the mask that led to the massively viral video. It was Candace Payne's infectious laugh that won everyone over. Every time she opened her mouth and the sound effect growl was triggered, Candace authentically and beautifully laughed hysterically. And we all laughed with her.

It wasn't professionally produced. It wasn't scripted. There wasn't time to get hair and makeup on point. And the chosen set was nothing more than the front seat of the family van.

And yet, with countless reactions and shares on this one 4-minute video, we recognized that live video had arrived.

Introduction

How We Got Here...
And What We've Got Here

Vintage commercials are a blast. Children hold up glasses of Ovaltine as though they'd just been given an ice cream sundae. Camel used to run a print ad in which an older gentleman in a white coat held up a cigarette. The headline? "More doctors smoke Camels than any other cigarette." There are entire websites dedicated to dated and sexist advertising pitching vacuum cleaners and cookware to 1950s housewives.

If you ever want to know just how much things have changed within living memory, just take a walk through those old commercials. They feel like another world.

But while the content of commercials has changed almost beyond recognition over the last sixty-odd years, until recently one aspect of advertising had remained the same. It interrupted. You'd turn the page in a magazine expecting to find the next article and you'd see a full page ad for a '57 Chevrolet, "sweet, smooth and sassy." You'd be listening to your favorite radio show and in the middle of some dramatic scene; you'd get a jingle for Fluffo from Proctor and Gamble, "the first new shortening in forty years."

Television was no better. Channels were built to hold advertising and content was pushed around the ads to keep people watching. No 1950s cowboy could ever get his man without some other man first telling viewers about the appeal of Kelloggs' "candy-sweet" Sugar Smacks.

That hasn't changed. Magazines, even when you've paid the subscription rate, are still filled with advertising. You might have to swipe your finger across a screen now to get to the article you want, but the ads are still there... and still in the way. Without the commercial breaks, a season of *24* would only have been eighteen hours long. No wonder Jack Bauer managed to get through the longest day of his life so easily: while you were watching commercials for headache pills and SUVs, the counter-terrorism agent was able to get a full-night's sleep.

The arrival of online advertising didn't bring an improvement—at least not initially. Banner ads became so common and so intrusive, forcing users to read around them and click past pop-ups and pop-unders, that as many as a quarter of all US Internet users are now said to use ad blockers to help them reach their content more easily.

That battle for attention is a challenge for audiences, for advertisers and for content producers. If audiences can avoid the ads, whether through an ad blocker, a quick swipe or a commercial-free pirated download, publishers will lose income. Without an audience, advertisers will struggle to inform the public about the qualities of their products. And without the content that advertising subsidizes, in the long run, those audiences will have nothing to watch, read or listen to.

It's a fight that has been raging since advertising began. Advertisers have always started with the assumption that no one would choose to see a sales message. They've always believed that content producers such as television channels, radio shows and newspapers should do the job of attracting the audience. They can then jump on stage, steal those audiences' attention for a few seconds and hold it just long enough to show their product before making way again for the game show or the rest of the article.

What changed that approach was the second wave of online advertising.

The first wave of online advertising had been defined by Google. Users would come to Google to search for information, and the company would sell space alongside those search results to related companies. In effect, the search giant's business model was little different than that used by the Yellow Pages, the company it all but killed. For a fee, businesses could make their listings more prominent to people looking for the services or products they offered.

Even when Google expanded to place its AdSense units on any Web page, the principal was the same. Audiences would come for the content and advertisers would butt in with their sales messages. Google was smart enough to be able to match the ads to the subject of the Web page but nothing had really changed. We were—and are—still reading around the ads.

The second wave of online advertising laid the foundation for something entirely new.

Facebook started with the same strategy that advertising had always followed but it added better demographic targeting. While Google showed ads that matched people's needs, Facebook was able to match ads to people themselves. They could analyze people's tastes and preferences and show them goods and services that they knew they'd like. That made the ads much more interesting to audiences and much more cost-effective for advertisers but the real innovation was what happening around the ads. Instead of content made by television producers, newspaper journalists and professional creatives, the content was being made by the users themselves. Brands were slipping their ads into users' news streams in exactly the same way that they had always put their messages into other people's content, but the content itself had changed dramatically.

It didn't take long before those brands realized that if users would follow content made by their friends and family, they might just follow content made by brands they liked too, content that was professionally made and entertaining but had a strong if subtle sales message. Those companies wouldn't need the giant sums that companies have to spend on cinematic Superbowl commercials. They just needed enough funds for a decent marketing firm... or a millennial graduate with a good grounding in social media and basic graphic design. Facebook gave them stats that let them track results and see which kind of content was working. Conferences, publications and experts watched what those big brands were doing, analyzed their campaigns and shared the results, allowing anyone to create effective social media marketing campaigns.

In a short space of time, advertising had started to change. Instead of satisfying itself with interrupting other people's content, brands were producing their own content—and people were choosing to watch it.

Sure, that content was still mostly seen in news feeds, in between pictures of a nephew's birthday party and a shared article from a newspaper. But this was branded sales content that viewers had *chosen* to see. Brands were no longer interrupting people who didn't really want to see them. They were delivering messages to people who wanted to hear from them and had made a choice to hear from them. Facebook was still selling ads, allowing brands to put their sales messages in the news streams of people who hadn't chosen to receive those messages but who might like them anyway, but brands were beginning to realize that their markets wanted a relationship with *them*. They weren't just interested in buying their products or learning about how many miles to the gallon the new model could do. They wanted to feel involved with the brand. They wanted it to be a part of their lives in the same way they were involved with their nephew's birthday party and their friend's political opinions.

The door to a close attachment was wide open. All they had to do was walk in.

So social media content improved. Brands improved their social media content. Short posts gave way to professional images. Those images gave way to videos. When users logged in to Facebook, as nearly one and a quarter *billion* people now do every day, they see content from their favorite brands, and as long as that content is good and entertaining they enjoy it. They even share it with their friends: to entertain them but also to show off their own taste and demonstrate how they see themselves.

But that viewing has still taken place according to the market's schedule. Brands would create content—recently, much of it has been video content—and make it available for their fans to see whenever they were ready. Often, that meant those fans never saw it at all. Users, now watching on mobile phones and tablets, might scroll past a video on their way to see pictures of their friend's vacation. Facebook too, came to realize that it needed to control access to audiences that brands had taken time, effort and expense to build. Facebook argues that each time a member opens the site, they could see around 1,500 different messages in their news stream. The company needed a way to make sure that members were seeing more of the messages they really wanted to see and fewer of the messages that meant less to them.

A filtering system that initially weighed the relationship of the post to the member, the range of actions taken on the post, and the amount of time since the post's publication has now morphed into a complex algorithm that takes into account no fewer than 100,000 different characteristics. Brands that had taken such efforts to build audiences then create the content that those audiences would enjoy seeing soon found that they were struggling to reach those followers.

One solution was to make better content. The more people shared, liked and viewed content the brands produced, the further it was likely to spread. But Facebook had a simpler solution: for a fee brands could bypass the filter. The more the brands paid, the more of their audience would see their posts. Fail to pay anything, and the brand might only reach as little as one or two percent of their followers.

That system has worked. It's what has made Facebook into a company that takes in $8 billion of ad revenue every year, or about 15 percent of all online advertising dollars. (Google still takes 50 percent or about $30 billion a year.)

But what brands really needed was a form of content that was so enticing and so inviting; they wouldn't have to pay to put it in front of their followers. If they could make something that people would deliberately create time to consume —in the same way they clear their schedules to watch sports on a Saturday afternoon—they wouldn't have to give Facebook money to reach their audiences. The audiences wouldn't just choose to receive their content; they would choose *to come and see* their content.

Urgency can do that. Sports fans set aside time to watch games live because the experience of watching a recorded game is different to watching it as it happens. They have only one chance to watch a game live so they make sure that they take that chance.

The ability to offer audiences live content would have been powerful enough alone to pull some of a brand's audiences to its content. But what if that content was even better than a live broadcast? What if it could also deliver live participation? Instead of just sitting on the sofa with a beer and a bag of pretzels, audiences could actually take part in the event they were watching. It would be like a cooking demonstration in a supermarket or a book reading by a famous author in a bookstore followed by questions from fans. It wouldn't appeal to everyone in a brand's audience—just most people who buy an author's book don't go out of their way to hear the author do a reading—but the people who found the brand most appealing wouldn't want to miss it.

Brands wouldn't have to pay to reach their most dedicated customers. And those customers would be rewarded for their dedication by exclusive content that delivered a memorable and unique brand experience.

In 2015, that solution came from Facebook itself. The company announced that it was rolling out live video to a select group of users. Instead of creating a video then uploading it for people to see, brands would be able to pick a time and broadcast live. Audiences could also use the comments to interact with the people on the screen and use "likes" and other reactions to show the brands how much they were enjoying what they were watching.

Once the show was over, other people could watch the video on the platform but they wouldn't be able to participate, and the event wouldn't have the same degree of urgency. Only people who made the time to watch the live broadcast would get the unique experience and the chance to interact with the people on the other side of the screen.

The difference between the video uploads that Facebook had long offered and the new live video looked small but it was actually a huge step. After giving brands an opportunity to create the audience-grabbing content that they had previous left to television channels and radio stations, *Facebook was now giving them the means to make that content unmissable.*

Now, this idea wasn't entirely original. Facebook wasn't the first to offer live video. Live streaming had been available on the Internet for some time. But Facebook's adoption of the format meant that for the first time brands could be certain that their streams would actually be able to reach audiences. Now it was worth putting in the effort to create live video because that live video would be shown in a venue filled with people.

Over the following year, Facebook expanded from its initial restricted group the list of publishers who could create live video. It even set aside $50 million to pay celebrities including Deepak Chopra, Kevin Hart, and NFL quarterback Russell Wilson to create content and publish it on the platform. Buzzfeed alone received $3 million. In April 2016, the company was happy enough with the results and felt enough confidence that its publishers had set strong examples to be able to roll out Facebook Live to everyone.

Other social media companies though, had been watching Facebook's experiments with live video closely. In December

2016, Twitter finally merged Periscope, a live video platform that it had purchased a year earlier, into its own app. In the same month, Instagram announced that it too would roll out live video to all its US users.

Brands have suddenly found themselves with a choice of live video platforms that they can use to share urgent, interactive and unmissable content with their audiences.

In this guide, we're going to look in detail at where live video has come from. We'll explore its early days on platforms like Ustream and show what social media giants have taken from those early successes and what they have added to them.

We'll then look at how live video can help both personal and business brands. We'll discuss the messages it can convey, the relationships that it can forge between brands and customers, and the potential that it can offer businesses and individuals who are willing to experiment and learn.

The following chapter will dive into the detail. Each of the different live video functions has different characteristics and offers different features. We'll look at what those features and functions offer, and when and how to make the most of them.

Finally, we'll go out into the real world and examine some case studies. We'll look at what some of the biggest brands are doing with live video, what they're getting right, what they're getting wrong, and what you can learn from their experience.

What we won't do in this report is look specifically at the various apps themselves. Live video is changing daily. New features are being released, the apps are being updated, and functionalities are being broadened. We have already seen the first experiments in live 360 degree video. By the time you've finished reading this report, there's a good chance that the live video function on your phone will have already changed.

Instead, we'll focus on those features and principles that underlie live video, the buttons you'll be pushing as you create your live content and the techniques that you'll be using. Let's start by seeing where we've come from.

Chapter 1

The Rapid Development Of Live Video Technology

L ive video might now be associated with branding and business-building but its origins were much nobler. Ustream, the first large-scale platform to allow users to broadcast video live across the Internet, was formed in 2007 by Brad Hunstable and John Ham. The pair had met at West Point and served together in the military for five years, completing foreign deployments and rising to the rank of captains. When they set up their company, they invited General Wesley Clark to join the advisory board. In December 2007, when Ustream was little more than a promising startup, the company developed a plan to send webcams to soldiers serving in Iraq so that they could livestream to their families over Christmas. The military nixed that idea for security reasons but servicemen and women who already had access to webcams were able to communicate with their families using the video streaming service.

The two West Point graduates weren't the only ones with the idea of turning offices (and barracks) with webcams into broadcast studios. The same year saw three other platforms launch, each offering a similar service though each had a slightly different edge. Mogulus, which rebranded as Livestream in 2009, began offering custom channel pages that often streamed concerts (the Foo Fighters were early adopters, broadcasting a live performance from their studio in Los Angeles.) The company has since morphed into a complete live video production service selling hardware as well as production solutions.

Also in 2007, Justin Kan attached a webcam to his baseball cap and broadcast his life online non-stop. The real-life Truman Show led to the launch of Justin.tv, a platform that allowed anyone to take part in what he called "lifecasting," the sharing of their life on video to anyone who wanted to watch it. The idea had limited appeal even in the age of reality TV. Justin.

tv folded in 2014 and relaunched as Twitch.tv, a platform that now live streams video games. Instead of watching people eating their breakfasts, the platform has nearly ten million active users who tune in daily to watch more than two million people broadcast their spellcasting and first person shooting every month. And in Europe, Bambuser was launching a similar, rival service.

That first wave of live video had three characteristics that would limit its appeal as technology advanced.

First, the hardware was clumsy. Justin Kan's early attempt at live streaming depended on a specially designed system that attached a webcam from a hat to a laptop held in a backpack. Today, he could have used his iPhone to broadcast effortlessly. Other platforms relied on webcams on computers, which restricted the kind of content that producers could easily broadcast. While bands could use all sorts of smart hardware to share their content, individuals were stuck sitting in front their computers in their bedrooms with a static camera. It didn't make for the most interesting viewing experience even though Facebook's rollout of live video for desktops suggests it still has some appeal.

Second, audiences had to make a special effort and really go out of their way to watch those videos. They had to visit sites that were unfamiliar and sift through lots of content of dubious quality in order to find a channel they might find interesting. Few people would do that on the off chance they'd strike gold. When brands did turn to Ustream, they had to tell their audiences where they were and how to find them on a website their audiences might never have used.

And that website was often in the study or the bedroom, or wherever the home computer happened to be located. It was a little like a television station telling an audience that the favorite show would be on Channel 53 but they could only watch it upstairs in their bedroom while everyone else was watching *Big Brother* in the living room.

And third, watching the videos was a solitary business. Audiences would have sat alone, with no way to communicate with the publisher or with other viewers. There was no interaction. The first wave of live video might have had a new urgency and it might have produced content that audiences might want to see but it still demanded both a special effort and passivity on behalf of audience members.

Ustream, the stronger of that first wave of live video platforms, is still around. The company was bought by IBM in January 2016 for a reported $130 million. IBM is said to be planning to combine the live video platform with a video management company it had already purchased, a video storage company it bought a few months earlier and a large-file transfer tool that it bought in late 2013. The aim is to offer a complete cloud-based video service for enterprises. Ustream might just be on the way to finding a dedicated audience at last.

The second live video wave came nearly eight years after the format launched, and it was spearheaded by two companies that were able to take advantage of the development of mobile devices to solve both the hardware problem and the accessibility challenge. While the first wave of businesses had relied on webcams stuck in offices (or attached to a baseball cap), the spread of cameras on mobile devices into everyone's pockets freed live video from static backgrounds and four walls. And with everyone now watching photos and videos on their phones, users were able to watch those live streams wherever they happened to be.

The development of mobile devices made the production of live video content easier and more interesting than it had ever been, and it made it much more convenient for audiences to access that content.

While a sprinkling of mobile live video apps began springing up prior to 2015, Spring of that year saw the launch of both Meerkat and Periscope. In a breakout battle, these two companies offered a very similar service: a live video feature that was tied to Twitter. Only one of the companies, though, would make it into 2017... and even that business would survive mostly as part of Twitter itself.

Meerkat was the first out of the gate, making a splash at the 2015 SxSW. Created by Ben Rubin, a 27-year-old Israeli architecture graduate, the app would start tweeting as soon as it went live, alerting a user's Twitter followers that someone they knew was broadcasting. Brands and individuals didn't have to plan their broadcasts. They could be spontaneous, share an interesting event that they happened to see at the time and still reach an audience. While Facebook was still keeping live video for celebrities and publishing companies, Meerkat made live video available to everyone.

The app racked up 150,000 users within a couple of weeks. In the same way that Twitter had won the love of SxSW users in 2007, keeping everyone informed of the best parties and the presentations that were making the biggest waves, so Twitter users eight years later found themselves using Meerkat to broadcast the events through their phones to their followers.

It was a simple idea, and one that Twitter should have implemented itself. In fact, the company had every intention of adding a live video feature, and it wasn't pleased to find a competitor already in place. Just as Meerkat was building traction at SxSW, Twitter pulled the rug from under it by cutting off the app from its social graph. People could still tell their Twitter contacts when they were streaming but new users wouldn't be added. It was a fatal blow that would slowly kill the app. By October 2016, Meerkat would be out of the live-streaming game.

Mark Zuckerberg ©
April 8, 2016

Today we're launching Facebook Live for everyone -- to make it easier to create, share and discover live videos

Live is like having a TV camera in your pocket. Anyone with a phone now has the power to broadcast to anyone in the world. When you interact live, you feel connected in a more personal way. This is a big shift in how we communicate, and it's going to create new opportunities for people to come together.

I'll be going live myself around 10:30am PT today and I'll answer some of your questions about the new product. Join me!

Twitter though, was developing its own plans. At the same time that it was killing Meerkat, the company announced that it had bought Periscope.

That app had been founded less than a year earlier by Keyvon Beykpour and Joe Bernstein who had the idea while they were traveling in 2013. When demonstrations broke out in Instanbul's Taksim Square, Beykpour used Twitter to follow what was happening but was frustrated that he couldn't see the demonstrations for himself in real time. "It just occurred to me, there were so many smartphones out there, why wasn't there a way for me to ask who else was out there what was happening there?" he told *Business Insider* in March 2015.

Beykpour, a graduate of Stanford University, had already sold one start-up, offloading TerriblyClever to the education company Blackboard. He was soon able to raise seed funding from angel investors who included Scott Belsky of Adobe. Belsky would describe the app as a teleportation device capable of putting anyone anywhere.

When Beykpour met Jessica Verrilli, a fellow Stanford alumna and Twitter's Director of Corporate Development and Strategy, for coffee and showed her what he had been building, Verrilli was impressed enough to introduce him to Twitter's then-CEO Dick Costolo and the company's co-founder Jack Dorsey. The Twitter executives quickly saw the app's value, and won a bidding war, paying an amounted said to be between $75 million and $120 million for the app.

That's a remarkable sum for an app that was less than a year old, still had relatively few users, and was certainly a long way from any form of monetization. But it had many of the basic features that we've already come to expect from live video.

Notifications told followers when someone was broadcasting. Hearts gave people a way to show their appreciation as the video was being shot. Going live was as simple as touching a button, entering a title and choosing an audience. It was all remarkably simple.

Having bought Periscope, Twitter was largely content to keep the two apps separate. While it was possible to broadcast from Periscope to Twitter, the parent company didn't yet have a native way to broadcast live video itself. That changed at the end of 2016 when Facebook suddenly parked its tank on Twitter's lawn.

The history of Facebook has been a movement from text posts to visual content. Mark Zuckerberg has been clear that he believed video would be the most popular form of content and he has gone out of his way to encourage that content. The platform favors native video when calculating organic reach—the audience a post can reach before payment. Facebook's first experiments with live video came in August 2015, around the same time that Meerkat was in terminal decline and about half a year after Twitter had bought Periscope. After rolling out live video first to celebrities then to select journalists, quietly paying them to set a standard, it began opening the feature to general users in January 2016. A number of iPhone users in the US were the first to play with live video then Android users got in on the act, and finally Facebook live become available universally on December 8, 2016.

As you might expect from a company with the resources of Facebook, the platform's live video feature is no budget offering. Like Periscope, the basic features are simple enough. Select the icon on the Facebook app, and you'll be able to enter a title for the video and choose an audience. Followers receive a notification that someone they know is broadcasting. They can share their reactions as the video is progressing, and they can also write comments, adding a level of interaction both with other viewers and with broadcasters themselves.

So far, so familiar… and so awesome. Initially, Facebook's big contribution to the development of live video wasn't the feature itself or the way that it worked, but the size of the audience. With well over a billion people on the platform every month, brands didn't need to pull customers towards them as they had previously needed to do during a live video. They were able to go directly to the audience itself. They could ping their customers' phones at any time and invite them to open an app they're used to opening every day anyway. They weren't just making a live television ad. They were offering their audience a live, prime-time television ad with interaction and a direct, physical nudge that made it as difficult to ignore as a telemarketing call.

Since that first roll-out Facebook has piled on more features. Tints and filters, an idea borrowed from Instagram, might be rarely used but they can make the videos look more interesting. Viewers can invite their friends to join them as they're watching, helping broadcasters build large audiences at a faster rate.

In January 2017, Facebook released six new Facebook Live tools and features. Pages can now appoint people to broadcast on their behalf. So a company could allow a number of employees to broadcast an event without making them page admins, giving audiences different views of the same event. A concert, for example, could allocate broadcast privileges to different performers, giving audiences multiple behind-the-scenes videos shot by band members and the crew. Broadcasters can now also pin the best comments to the bottom of the live broadcast, giving them more power to influence the conversation. After the video has finished, a permalink makes it easier to bring audiences to watch them again, and Facebook has eased the restrictions on cross-posting to different pages. In an odd step back, aimed largely at vloggers, Facebook Live is also now available on laptops and desktops, and broadcasters can also schedule their broadcasts in advance, ensuring that followers receive reminders as they're preparing for the broadcast.

But there are two features on Facebook Live that most other live video platform has yet rolled out, and which will prove particularly important. First, Facebook Live delivers detailed stats. Once broadcasters can see exactly how many people tuned in and when they reached their peak audience, they'll be able to improve the content they offer. Those stats will go a long way towards ensuring a continuous improvement in live video quality.

And in February 2017, Facebook announced that it was expanding its beta test of Ad Breaks in Facebook Live to additional profiles and pages in the US that have at least 2,000 followers and reach 300 or more concurrent viewers. Advertisers are able to upload video ads and bids to Facebook which "quickly" runs an auction to allocate the ads to live videos. The company has worked with Collective Press and with Univision to produce eCPMs 52 percent higher than other monetization partners.

After at least four minutes of broadcasting, publishers will see a dollar icon on their Live composer window. They can then tell their audiences that they'll be right back, push the button and take an ad break that will last up to 20 seconds. They won't be able to take another break for at least five minutes. The broadcaster earns a share of the revenue.

Ad-sharing in live video is a major step. It will go a long way towards incentivizing more brands to use live video, and to use it in a way that's more effective. Facebook is still experimenting with the system and it will take some time before publishers and advertisers figure out the best way to combine revenue generation with audience retention. It's a whole new world.

So Twitter has now merged Periscope into its platform. In fact, this author sees Periscope eventually disappearing completely into Twitter. So as to not cause confusion, whenever you see me mention Periscope you may also think of how the functionality is integrated with Twitter.

In the midst of this Facebook is racing ahead, piling on features that make it easier than ever for broadcasters to engage the massive audiences they can reach on the site—and even earn from them. In fact, as of Spring 2017 Facebook announced that 1 in 5 videos posted to the site are now live videos. That's 20% of all videos in less than the two years the feature has been available.

Instagram hasn't been left out. The photo-sharing app that saw off Yahoo's Flickr has been struggling in recent years to compete with Snapchat. In November 2016, the company announced a new weapon to keep Snapchat at bay: Live Video.

Instagram's version differs from the versions offered by Facebook and Twitter in a number of different ways. First, the user experience is different from the others. As well as hitting an icon to bring up the live video option, users can also swipe right from anywhere in the feed. Once you start broadcasting,

Instagram notifies "some" close friends and displays a Live tag on the Stories bubble at the top of followers' feeds. The Stories feed on the Explore tab will also display live videos currently being broadcast so publishers should be able to pick up some random viewers. Audiences can comment and send hearts, and as on Facebook, broadcasters can pin comments to guide the conversation.

But while Periscope started by allowing live videos to be rewatched up to 24 hours after broadcast, and Facebook is making it as easy as possible to share recordings of live broadcasts, Instagram has moved in the opposite direction. Taking a leaf out of Snapchat's book, Instagram makes live videos temporary. As soon as the stream stops, the video is over and there is no replay option. You are able to download the video, however. But by the time this book is published, that could all change. That's how fast things are moving!

It's a risky strategy. On the one hand, it gives each broadcast greater urgency: miss the video and it's gone. It may also encourage more frequent uses of live video. Broadcasters will need to go live several times to reach their audiences. But it will also discourage broadcasters from putting great effort into their live broadcasts when the chance to see them is so limited. Instagram Live might be useful for behind- the-scenes shoots or for addressing small groups of people but the more complex live broadcasts, and those that can benefit from a longer life, are more likely to find their home on Facebook.

The history of live video on the Internet is short. But even in that limited space of time, we've seen exciting apps rise and fall, and we've seen giant platforms with enormous audiences roll out sophisticated products that should attract the attention of any brand.

And that history hasn't stopped. While the products on offer, and particularly Facebook Live, are likely to dominate for a while, a space this dynamic is full of surprises. I've predicted for some time that Snapchat will roll out its version of live video as the competition for EPM (Eyeballs per Minute) is what is driving the competition between apps. Instagram has already said that it's considering making its live function available to private groups. There's plenty more to come.

Those features will be important but what really makes a live video successful is the content the brand puts into each broadcast. Despite the changes in features and functionality which will continue to evolve, what you need to know about how live video can enhance your brand and grow your business will remain the same. Let's take a look at these evergreen aspects of live video next.

Chapter 2

Live Video For Personal Branding And Business

Whenever a new marketing channel is laid out between businesses and markets, the first reaction of executives is always the same: they scratch their heads and they wonder what they're supposed to do with it. They also hope that this is something they can just ignore. What they've been doing until now has been working for them. If they can keep on doing what they've been doing, and continue earning money in the same way, they'll be happy.

They'll hope that while their competitors are busy being distracted by the new marketing toy, they'll be able to expand their business using methods that they already know and that are tried and trusted.

Sometimes it works. Businesses that put money and time into their MySpace pages would have been left feeling pretty foolish when the platform collapsed. But those adventurous companies would also have been the first to try Facebook —and they would have been the first to benefit from that platform's explosive growth. While their competitors were wondering why their Yellow Pages phone calls were drying up, they would have been getting to grips with building follower lists and understanding Facebook advertising. By not allowing themselves to be left behind, they're able to race ahead.

Adventurous companies are now taking a similar attitude to live video. They're experimenting. They're trying different kinds of content. They're playing with the features. They're testing different ways of promoting their broadcasts, and they're working with the platforms to figure out which approaches work best.

Later in this report, we'll look in detail at a number of case studies drawn from businesses that have made progress with live video. In this chapter, we're going to focus on some of the results. We'll begin with storytelling and where your content will originate from. We'll look at the main types of content that both personal brands and businesses have used with live video and we'll explore what they mean for businesses as a whole. We'll then look at some of the issues that businesses have to consider as they're planning their live video content.

What Kind of Content Makes for Good Live Video?

You pick up your mobile device, launch the app you'll use to go live, push the "go live" button and... now what?

You most certainly want to say something, and each of your broadcasts should have a central theme. Just like a television sitcom episode that tells a story and resolves in thirty minutes (well, twenty-two minutes and eight minutes of commercials!), you'll want to tell your story in a way that is satisfying and engaging for your viewers.

In case you didn't pick up on it, I just called you a Storyteller. We are all storytellers, and our businesses, products and services all tell a story. Your job as the live video broadcaster is to tell your story.

There are four basic kinds of stories, and once you understand them you'll likely discover that going live is much easier than you had anticipated.

1. Teach Me Something

Clickbait Events

When Facebook set aside $50 million to pay well-known publishers to create content that would set a standard for others to follow, it's not certain that blowing up a watermelon with rubber bands was what they had in mind. But in April 2016, that's exactly what Buzzfeed did. The site filmed a pair

of employees wearing protective clothing as they added one rubber band after another to a watermelon until... 690 rubber bands later... the melon exploded, sending bits of fruit everywhere.

The video ran for around 45 minutes, and at its peak was watched by 807,000 viewers at the same time. Since the broadcast, total views have numbered more than 11 million.

For the development of live video it was a seminal moment. The previous years had seen the sudden spread of clickbait headlines promising readers that they "wouldn't believe what happened next!" Many of those headlines had already started to lose their power but this video showed that simple, dramatic content with a single payoff could pull in audiences.

It didn't matter that the video contained nothing of any importance. It wasn't a live broadcast from a protest in the capital of some troubled country as the founders of Periscope had hoped to show. It wasn't a product demonstration or a studio interview as brands would have considered when they first heard of live video. It was two people having fun. It was the kind of weird, silly experiment that students would want to perform in a frat house if they were told they wouldn't have to clean up the mess.

It was funny and packed with suspense. Viewers could watch without knowing whether the next rubber band would be the one that sent bits of watermelon flying around the office. They'd stay for just one more band, worried that if they turned away now, they'd just miss the move that made the explosion. It was Jenga on steroids. (The 10 million or so people who watched the video after it was broadcast are more likely to have watched a few minutes then fast-forwarded to the last seconds.)

So a live video that is, let's face it, a little silly, could still get large numbers of viewers. The first question it raises then, is what does it do for the company that broadcasts it? For Buzzfeed, the simplest answer is that it justified the $3 million that Facebook paid it. The website was able to point to the video's viewing figures and show Mark Zuckerberg that he was getting his money's worth. Zuckerberg in turn would have been more than happy with the massive viewing figures and the large discussions of Facebook Live that followed.

But clearly the Buzzfeed brand benefitted as well. The 11 million people who saw the video got to see the company's name and they came to associate Buzzfeed with fun video content. That fit Buzzfeed's general direction. Between the end of 2014 and September 2016, Buzzfeed's share of revenue generated by video rose from 15 percent to more than 50 percent. According to *The New York Times* the company expects 75 percent of its income to derive from video content by the end of 2018. The watermelon video also came at a time when the company was separating its news content from its entertainment content. The video went a long way towards branding itself as a source of entertainment for younger viewers.

As a model, it's not one that's hard to follow. Live clickbait videos need to be silly, the kind of thing viewers would like to do but dare not. They should suggest that something dramatic could happen at any moment. And they should match the rest of the content produced by the brand. *The New York Times* might have reported on Buzzfeed's watermelon-smashing antics but if they had done something similar they would have hurt their serious brand.

If you're producing live videos with entertaining content, the rest of the company must have a link to entertainment.

Straight To Camera

When cameras were first attached to computers, they could only shoot one thing: the person in front of the lens. That's

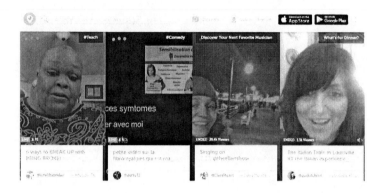

still the easiest thing in the world to film, and to the person broadcasting, it's may well be the most interesting thing they want to show. With as many as a million selfies taken every day, it's not surprising that one of the most common forms of live video is little more than a live, moving selfie.

That can be useful, especially for personal brands. It takes very little effort to hold a phone, hit the broadcast icon and talk to whoever happens to be online at the time. Those small points of contact go a long way towards building a connection with audiences and with followers. Personal brands thrive on a sense that the audience has a friend who can help them achieve their goals. A live video shot straight to camera can feel like a quick phone call. It's as though a friend has called them up to see how they're doing and offer advice. Even the small audience that a spontaneous live broadcast will generate can work in favor of the brand. The audience might be small, but it's privileged. They're getting exclusive help from someone they admire, and they're getting it for free. And while the advice might be valuable, providing it costs next to nothing. Personal brands can talk to the camera while they're taking a walk, working out in the gym or eating their breakfast. Because these kinds of live videos really are as easy as making a phone call—you only need to be able to hold the phone, or prop it up so that it won't fall—it's something you can do at any time. In effect, Facebook, Periscope and all the other platforms have given personal brands not just a live video platform but a direct phone number to manage a conference call with their audiences at any time they want.

But they're not the sort of thing that many businesses can easily do. Companies that are strongly identified with their owner might be able to make use of a broadcast made straight to camera but when the business is more interesting than the person behind it, audiences will want to see the product and the company more than they'll want to see the manager or the founder. The owner of a retail store, for example, could use Periscope to tell customers about the products currently on sale, but what people watching will really want to see are the products themselves.

An alternative approach is to reverse the camera. Instead of pointing it at yourself, show your viewers what you can see. GoPro has integrated its cameras with Periscope, allowing you to broadcast from the top of your head or out of the window. While you might not be able to look into the screen to address your audiences, you will be able to give that audience a varied view and the moving camera that moviemakers prefer. It can make for a much more interesting experience. Some live video broadcasters who have experimented with videos broadcast direct to camera and videos shot while they were surfing have reported much higher engagement rates when they were riding the waves then when they were filming themselves walking on the beach.

You don't have to dismiss moving selfies, but don't get so caught up on them that you forget that people also want to see what's around you.

Go Behind The Scenes

Mark Zuckerberg ✔ was live.
February 21, 2016 · Facebook Mentions · ⊖

Live behind the scenes in Barcelona

3.7M Views

Should the public see how the sausages are made? If you're making sausages (or laws) probably not. Some things are best left unseen. But if we learned anything from the extras tacked on to special edition versions of DVDs, it's that there's a great deal of interest in how the things we love are put together. It's something that Mark Zuckerberg exploited before broadcasting a live Q&A session in Barcelona in 2016, and it's something

Academy.live

that fashion brands were doing as far back as 2015. That year's London Fashion Week saw companies including Burberry, TopShop, Louboutin and Versace using Periscope to show how the event was organized and how the big fashion companies prepare their collections.

Each of those companies benefited from the spread of the #LFW hashtag. Anyone interested in seeing the construction of the event could search for that hashtag and see different views of the same topic. That's one way to make the most of behind-the-scenes shooting, which is still one of the most common ways that brands make use of live video. When everyone is using the same hashtag, everyone benefits.

Shooting behind the scenes, though, raises a couple of important issues. First, it removes some of the magic. When paparazzi snap celebrities eating hot dogs and looking like everyone else, those stars lose some of their shine. It's part of the attraction for the public but it comes at a cost to the star who would rather the public only saw them when they looked their best. Any scene that you shoot behind the scenes has to look as professional and be as well-planned as the event itself. It has to match the tone of the main content.

So when DVDs include behind the scenes moments from movies, they're often introduced by a member of the cast who shows carefully selected parts of the set. We don't see actors learning their lines… or forgetting them on camera. Even the behind the scenes sequences have to stay on message. They're still part of the content itself.

Where they differ, though, is in who sees them—and that's the second important issue that a live video broadcast behind the scenes raises. Millions of people might watch a movie. Only a small percentage of those people would have bought the DVD. And only a small percentage of the people who bought the DVD would have been interested in the movie enough to stick around to watch the special features.

The people who watch these kinds of broadcasts are always the biggest fans, the people who just can't get enough. That's something to bear in mind when you're planning behind the scenes content. You're talking to people who know the language, who know the people and who understand what's going on. You can use jargon to show that you're part of the same crowd. You can geek out about technology and machinery important to your business. You can make use of the fact that you're not talking to regular customers; you're talking to your most engaged customers, the ones who know the most. It requires a shift in language and a more in-depth look at your topic but it should result in a close connection to customers who form a community around your business.

Live Interviews

One alternative strategy to filming a talking head—usually your own!—addressing an audience live online is to use two talking heads. If information from one expert is going to be interesting, then information from two experts should be twice as interesting.

And it's just as easy to do. Everyone knows people in their industry with whom they share an audience. You wouldn't want to promote a competitor but there's nothing wrong with introducing your audience to someone who sells a complementary product… especially if you know that they're going to introduce you to theirs in turn.

You can talk to a supplier, a member of your team, or anyone who would be interesting to the people who buy your products. You get to have a friendly chat, and your audience gets to benefit from that chat.

It's easiest when you're in the same room, and the most fun. You can interview someone in your office or in the lobby of a hotel at a conference. That personal connection makes for a warmer experience both for you and for the audience. But if you can't get together in person, there's no shortage of technological solutions that can let you broadcast two streams from two people in two different places.

In fact, you can go even further. Town hall meetings don't just have to be opportunities for angry constituents to shout at their representatives. They can also be opportunities for members of your audience to interview you live online. Crowdcast.io, for example, brings multiple people into the same stream. You can use it to create an online panel of experts and you can use it to generate a discussion that anyone can join and watch.

I'm presently utilizing a service called Belive.tv for my weekly interview show, Joel.LIVE. The platform has a free basic version that streams your live video direct to any Facebook page. As with all platforms, it's fun to kick the tires and see which best suit your needs. True to Facebook's constant testing of new features, they have rolled out its own version of dual-stream live video in limited release.

Corporate And Institutional Events

And finally, businesses put on all sorts of events: grand openings, bonanza sales, product launches, big announcements, and so on. All of those events are intended to reach audiences that are as large as possible. Before live video, they could only reach those people who happened to be in the location at the time. That's no longer the case. Now when you're organizing a publicity

event, it's possible to reach anyone... even when you're not announcing "just one more thing" and you don't have a hall full of reporters waiting on every word.

Even the government has already picked up on the value of live broadcasting its announcements. It allows their officials to skip the media, bypass reporters and talk directly to people who want to hear the information that's being shared.

For businesses, that's now a breeze, and you can combine the different kinds of live video content to create a complete show for audiences. So you can prepare for a live broadcast of a corporate event by showing what's happening behind the scenes and by interviewing the people behind the announcement such as the designers of the product or the owners of the store.

Academy.live

However you choose to do it, you get to expand your audience and introduce the event to as many people as you can attract.

Those five forms of content have proved to be the most commonly used so far on live video. But they're not the only forms of content that have been produced, and they're not the only ones that have to be produced. Fashion magazine *Grazia*, for example, worked with Facebook to broadcast the publication's editorial process. Viewers were invited to weigh in with their own feature ideas and even had the chance to be commissioned to produce them. Some of the items broadcast were staged events planned to entertain audiences in the same way as a chat show. The publication organized a debate about Brexit and brought in singer Craig David to perform live. That broadcast generated 250,000 views but it also showed that the publication had effectively created a television show that was part behind-the-scenes content and part free entertainment. It's complex and requires planning but it can be very effective.

It was also an experiment, and one that yielded a great deal of information about what works for live video audiences. It went some way towards answering some of the questions that live video broadcasters are going to need to ask.

Should Live Videos Be Long Or Short?

Grazia's answer to the optimal length for a live video broadcast was clear. "The lessons we learned are that half an hour to an hour is best for timings," editor Natasha Pearlman told *Digiday*. Longer videos allow time for word of mouth to spread on social media, boosting the view count as friends hit the Share button and bring in more viewers.

That's true for Facebook Live, and it's true in general for videos that require planning and effort to create. The success of Buzzfeed's watermelon explosion was no doubt due in part to people telling their friends on social media to come and check out what was happening on the company's Facebook page. The event took long enough—around 45 minutes—for both the suspense and the audience to build.

When you're trying to gather as large an audience as possible, that 30 to 60 minute length may well deliver the best return on your investment.

But those kind of long Facebook Live posts aren't the only type of content you can create. If a live video can be like a conference call with a small group of friends, it can also be short, and it's now easy enough for that short duration to be worthwhile. Not everyone has 45 minutes in the middle of a workday to sit and watch a video—let alone a video of an exploding watermelon.

One of the types of content that Facebook promotes for live video is a quick clip from a concert. That's a way for friends to share an experience with other friends who aren't with them at the time. There's no reason that personal brands and businesses can't do the same thing. Those short videos might be best shared on Periscope or Instagram (if you don't want them to last) rather than on Facebook. They won't have large audiences, but they'll require no planning and no effort, and they'll cement a close relationship with the people who see them. Shoot them often and at different times, and while you won't have a lot of people watching at once, you should be able to reach a large number of people.

The answer to whether live videos should be long or short then, is both. Long videos will bring in lots of people at the same time to see an event; short videos, shot frequently, will provide brief contact with lots of people separately and at little expense for either the broadcaster or the viewer.

Should Live Videos Be Planned Or Spontaneous?

The same principle that applies to the length of a broadcast also holds true for the planning. Buzzfeed's watermelon video appears to have been the result of careful thought. You can imagine the staff at the site sitting in an editorial meeting throwing ideas around until someone came up with the idea to explode a watermelon. Most people would have laughed, some would have rolled their eyes and someone would have decided: "Let's do it!" Then they would have had to think about what they needed, other than a watermelon and a giant pile of rubber bands. They would have thought about how they were going to let people know, and whether they should curate the comments. They would have needed to reserve a space, and choose two people willing to stand next to a large exploding fruit.

None of that would have taken a huge amount of effort. *Grazia's* entire editorial team decamped from Italy to London for its live video which it broadcast in collaboration with Facebook. That would have taken months planning, preparation and forethought. It would also have created a great deal of expense but the effort and the cost allowed the broadcaster to offer a large audience content that was as unique and complex as the articles in the magazine, but with extra participation.

It's effective, but again it's not the only way to create effective live video content. Pulling out your phone and talking when you feel like it can also be effective. It's different. A planned event will pull in lots of people who don't know you. A spontaneous broadcast will only reach a small number of the people who are already following you but it will cement your relationship with them.

You should be doing both. Plan complex, long broadcasts to widen your reach; use short, spontaneous broadcasts to deepen the connection whenever you have a spare minute.

How To Manage Interaction

One of the big innovations that live video has brought to communications is interaction. For the first time, a video broadcast isn't a one-way street. Audiences can send messages directly to the brand that the brand can see in real time. That makes a huge difference but the interaction isn't equal. Everyone sees the broadcaster, and everyone sees the comments. But the only person who is being *watched* is the person making the broadcast. And the only person who determines what the broadcast will contain is the brand making it. The flow of comments delivers options but it's still up to the brand to retain exercise control.

The simplest reaction to comments is to welcome people as they come in. Obviously, you can't welcome everyone; the first minutes of the video would be like a long credit roll before a film, and the rest of the broadcast would be filled with interruptions. But you can—and should—welcome some people as they join the broadcast. You don't even have to wait for comments to do that. Pick people at random from the notifications and say "hi." It's an easy way to make them feel special.

Once the broadcast is under way, though, you can pull them into the conversation. Julius Dein who made a name for himself by uploading videos of his magic tricks and gags to YouTube and Facebook, has used Facebook Live to give control to his audience. They tell him what to do and he goes and declares his love for a stranger or falls asleep on them on the subway. He uses comments to make the audience part of the act.

Any performer can do that. Singers can take requests. Comedians can shoot down hecklers. Athletes can accept challenges. This as close to interactive television as we've ever been! In fact, I believe live video is the real reality television.

You can also pin comments that you want to emphasize, which is a lot more effective than it sounds. You can think of pinning as another way to highlight. It makes the person who posted the comment feel special but it also guides the comments in the direction you want them to go. It shows people how you want them to react.

So if you were showing off a product in a live video and someone commented that they just bought it, pinning that comment would show others that they can—and should—do the same thing.

Comments do have a limitation though. While you can react to them in the video, you can only answer them in the comments while you're broadcasting if you're using a desktop; it's too difficult to thumb-type while a phone, and even typing on a keyboard doesn't make for the most entertaining videos.

You'll have to pick the best comments as the coming in and respond to them in real time. And once the broadcast is finished, you'll need to go over the comments and see if there are any issues that need addressing.

It's not the best solution. Ideally, you'd be able to assign an assistant to type replies during the broadcast, so that you can focus on the video itself and audiences have their questions answered while they're watching. Maybe that feature will find its way onto live video platforms soon.

Whenever marketers get a new toy to play with, they have to figure out how to make the most of it. They need to know how it works and what tricks they can perform with it. They experiment, ditch what doesn't work and do more of what does. Other marketers see what they're doing and copy them, and quickly some forms of content become standard. Even though live video is still new, that standardization has already started to happen. Brands are using videos shot live behind the scenes of companies and events, to offer a reliable insight into the way a favorite product is created. Interviews with a product designer or inventor allow users to ask their own questions and dig deeper into the creating of a loved product. Live broadcasts of corporate events widen audiences to people who can't be on site. And planned events are turning brands into real content creators who can build a connection with their audiences through urgency, entertainment and interaction.

The tools that brands are using to create that content are still limited though they are growing. We've already touched on some of them but in the next chapter, we're going to provide a rundown of the live video options already available on social media platforms and the tools that we can expect to see rolling out soon.

Chapter 3

Features To Find, Use And Expect When Live Video Broadcasting

L ive video is changing and growing fast. Just as brands are experimenting with content that attracts, keeps and engages audiences so social media platforms are figuring out which tools those brands need and which new options might allow them to produce better and more creative content.

New features are constantly being passed out to select users. Some of those features will find their way to general release. Others are likely to disappear after failing to gain traction in testing. But already a number of features have become baked into the format, some more useful than others… and a number of new exciting options are on the way. In this chapter, we're going to take a quick look at each of the main live video features, what they can do and how to use them.

Video Descriptions

Before a live video broadcast begins, you'll be asked to enter a name for the video. At the moment, that name is less important than the titles you put on other forms of content, such as blog posts. Those posts will face competition from a host of other articles with other headlines, and they can be read at any time. The most important description of a live video is the one that the social media platforms give it automatically in the notification: "live now."

Once the broadcast is over and the video is added to your video album, you can always go back and put in some keywords or make the title more clickbait-like. But when you're broadcasting, you want to go live as quickly as possible. Remember the title when you're finished broadcasting, and go back and clean it up. But there's little reason to sweat too hard over it as you're about to begin broadcasting.

Audience Selection

The other decision you'll need to make before you go live is who you want to allow to see your video. On Facebook, that means you can choose from one of your pre-arranged list of followers. Your broadcast can go to your personal profile timeline, a business page that you administer, a group you are a part of or an event.

In theory, that should be a valuable tool. You know how important list segmentation is to email marketing. Sending the right message to the right audience grouping increases clicks and responses. But the same principle doesn't apply to social media. Whether you're on Periscope, Instagram or Facebook, you want as many people to see your content as possible. Unless you've got a good reason to do otherwise—such as creating a live video for people for a list of social media followers who have bought a product or attended an event —you're going to want as many people to watch as possible.

The two features that you're offered before you start broadcasting are actually the two you want to think about the least.

Filters & Lenses

Instagram made filters indispensable and Snapchat showed the value of being able to put a funny mask of a dog over your face. But none of the live videos that have had the greatest success so far have been powered by filters, doodles or lenses. They've succeeded because what was happening on the screen was interesting.

It's good to know that these features are there, and if you think that a live video might be enhanced after broadcast by playing with how you or the screen looks, then have fun. But the reason that filters are so popular on Instagram is that they make bad pictures look good.

A live video with weak content won't be helped by a snazzy filter or a puppy dog mask. No one is going to watch a dull video for 45 minutes because it looks like a drawing. Experiment with these features but focus on the quality of the content that you're offering. They are best used if integrated with the content of your broadcast. For example, you are more likely to get away with wearing a funny cartoon graduation cap lense superimposed on your video if you have just received a diploma or certificate. Content is, and always will be, king.

Reactions

One of the really great advantages that live broadcasters have over traditional broadcasters is the instant feedback. As you're broadcasting, you'll be able to see the hearts rolling across the screen. It's like receiving constant applause as you're talking. Or rather, it's a bit like receiving applause as you're talking because audiences know when to applaud during performances—and speakers and performers know how to read those reactions. If a magician pulls a rabbit out of a hat and gets silence, he knows the crowd wasn't impressed and he puts the rabbit down.

But audiences are currently less certain when to react during a live broadcast. You'll get reactions as you're talking, and you'll get them as people join the audience. You might not get them as you're giving away valuable information even though that information is great because the audience is too busy making notes or too busy watching to remember to tap the button. Enjoy the reactions as they come in. Pay attention to when you get the most reactions and whether one video gets more reactions than another. But pay more attention to the comments. They're more important.

Comments

Comments are where it's all happening on live video. This is the killer feature. It's the closest we've come yet to interactive television. Those comments aren't just there to give the audience a way to say something nice about the brand. They're the conversation, and they'll help define the content you'll put in the live video.

You want to get as many people commenting as possible. You want to react to the comments you see coming in by answering questions and responding to the points people raise. You want to show that you're listening and you want to make the audience feel that they're involved in creating the experience and the brand.

If the broadcast is a success, you won't be able to respond to every comment but once it's over, you should take the time to go over the comments and see if there were any important issues that you missed. Those comments will contain some valuable data about your business and its relationship with its market.

Pinned Comments

Pinned posts have become a great way to promote a message that you want to emphasize on social media. Place them at the top of a Twitter or Facebook page, and they can tell audiences about a product you're selling or an event you're promoting.

Pinned comments do the same thing in live videos. But they do it with even more power. Because those comments are coming from users, they look like testimonials. Because they reward members of the audience, they encourage other members to make similar comments. And because anyone can make a comment during a broadcast, you can use them to turn a broadcast into a team event. While you're broadcasting, a member of your team write a comment that you pin can to guide the conversation.

While you're most likely just to pin comments that stand out, this is a feature with a great deal of potential.

Metrics

Live video's metrics might not be a feature that can be seen by audiences but they're vital for broadcasters. Periscope and Instagram still keep their metrics restricted to overall viewing figures, but Facebook has raced ahead with detailed breakdowns for page admins. Not only can you see the largest number of people watching at the same time, as well as the total number of unique viewers, views, ten-second views and average completion rate, you can also break those figures down by demographics and geography. You can see how many of your views came from shares instead of views on your page itself, a figure that will give you greater incentive to ask people to hit that share button.

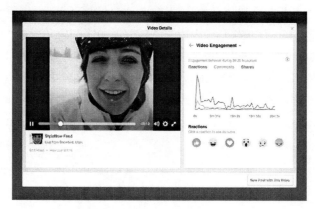

Best of all, you can see which moments in the video triggered the biggest reactions and the most comments and shares. Again, you'll need to be cautious with the Reactions line but once your Facebook Live broadcast is over, pull up those stats and check out what caused people to share and comment. Those metrics will help you to make your videos better and more engaging.

Expect this level of detail to expand to Periscope, Twitter and Instagram but until it does, make sure that you use those Facebook metrics to improve your live video across all platforms.

Repackaged Videos And Temporary Videos

Once a live broadcast is over, two things can happen to the video. It will both be saved and made available for more people to see in a recorded form. Or it will be deleted. Facebook and Periscope keep your live videos; Instagram doesn't (but they do allow you to download your video). Each of those options requires some thought, and should help to determine which platform you use for a particular broadcast.

In practice though, despite the extra urgency that Instagram offers, you're most likely to want to keep the videos and benefit from the extra views they can win after the broadcast. And if urgency is what you want in particular, you can always delete the video after the recording.

Instagram's temporary videos may have a use, especially for brands with big Instagram followings, but most brands will find themselves broadcasting their videos on Facebook and Twitter, and keeping them there.

Desktop Live

Facebook Live on desktops is something that brands need to be aware of, especially personal brands. It's going to be the easiest way to broadcast live. You'll be sitting in your office, at your desk, feeling completely comfortable, and you'll be able to talk directly with your audience. It will be the easiest and most enjoyable work task you do that day. You can even write comments as you're broadcasting, an improvement on mobile broadcasts.

If you don't have desktop live, you can still go live from your office. There's nothing to stop you from propping your phone against your monitor now, and hitting the live button.

You might well be able to come up with some good content from your office. You could offer some great professional advice, interview a colleague, and talk your audience through an issue or a product. But it's so easy; it can be dangerous to broadcast in a static setting. You must be able to carry the broadcast purely on the quality of your spoken content. Whether from inside an exhibit or outside at a city fair, mobile broadcasts are often more interesting. The audience can see stuff happening. The background changes. It's dynamic. There's a whole world of content options taking place outside the walls of your office; choosing to use your webcam cuts you off from those options.

It's likely that you'll be using desktop live just because it's so convenient, but be careful not to let it dominate your broadcasts.

Live Contributors

When Facebook Live first rolled out, only the page admins could broadcast. Facebook has since introduced a new class of admin called Live Contributors. They can broadcast from the page without having any of the other admin privileges.

It's not something that's going to be too useful for many brands but it does point to the direction that Facebook thinks live video is going to take. Live Contributors are likely to be video marketing people hired by large corporations specifically to manage live video content. Facebook expects live video to become more professional. It expects the marketing firms responsible for a big brand's social media campaign to want to give access to live video makers while still retaining control over the page's overall messaging. If you can see a Live Contributor option on your Facebook page, understand that it's there for a reason; it's a plug that allows big companies to install their professional services.

Multiple Person Broadcasts

It's already possible to broadcast simultaneously from different locations using Belive.tv, Crowdcast.io, Smiletime or any number of additional applications which already exist, but Facebook is said to have been testing group broadcasts since the summer of 2016. The idea is to allow two people in different locations to hold a public conversation.

That's clearly going to be useful. Interviews can make for great live content and you don't have to wait for Facebook to make that easy for you. You can already experiment with interview content and see how your audience reacts. Get together with a friend or a colleague, put your phone on a selfie stick and broadcast your chat. Invite the audience to ask their own questions. Tell them to share the video.

But bear in mind that a video of two people sitting in two different offices doesn't look exciting. It's not very visual. So mix it up. Interview a colleague as he's sitting on a bench by a lake or as you take a walk through a wood. Multi-person broadcasts don't have to be multi-office broadcasts.

Live Video Waiting Rooms

Perhaps the most interesting development currently taking place in live video is waiting rooms. Broadcasters have a problem: they don't want to go live until they know people are watching, but no one will watch until they're live. As part of the professionalization of live video, Facebook has rolled out both scheduled broadcasts and "waiting rooms" that show content until the broadcast itself begins. Scheduling is available for setting up a broadcast on a business page. Essentially you set a time for the video to begin and get everything ready. Audiences may click a button to be notified when the broadcast commences. It's going to be like producing your own television show.

It won't be spontaneous but it should make for live videos that are prepared, professional... and that have an audience.

You've probably noticed that many of these features are being developed by Facebook. That doesn't mean that other platforms are sitting on their hands. They're not. But Facebook is currently the most creative... and it has the biggest audience. You might well prefer to use Periscope to broadcast news events on Twitter, and Instagram to show the sun setting to people who love your Instagram photography but most marketing-related live videos are likely to go out on Facebook. That's where the audiences are that's where many of the most innovative features are currently being tested.

Chapter 4

Live Video Case Studies

L ive video hasn't been around for long but already businesses large and small are experimenting. They're trying out different formats, lengths, content and degrees of interaction, and they're playing with the features that the platforms are offering. In this chapter, we're going to look at some of the most important experiments in live video that have taken place so far and what they mean.

National Post Reporters Versus Homer Simpson

In April 2016, reporter Victor Ferreira wrote a story for the Canadian *National Post* about Cheesefest. The annual

National Post 🌐 was live.
April 19, 2016 ·

Watch National Post staffers try to break Homer Simpson's record and eat more than 64 slices of American cheese.

eating competition attempts to break the record of 64 slices of American cheese set by Homer Simpson in season five of the Fox TV show. The competition started as a dare between a group of teenagers and developed into a yearly event. Contestants eat one slice of Kraft cheese at a time, are scored by a manager, are allowed to drink water… and if they feel a need to throw up, there are no penalties. It was a fun story for the *Post*.

Having published the article though, the *Post* tried to promote it with a live video. A group of reporters joined Victor

Ferreira on Facebook Live in their own attempt to beat Homer Simpson's cheese-eating contest.

It wasn't pretty… and neither were the results. Although the video generated over 200 comments, total viewing figures, even after the event, barely topped 11,000.

The *National Post* was clearly trying to copy Buzzfeed's watermelon success story. It had seen a bizarre food-centered video break the Internet and it figured it could do the same. It didn't happen. So what went wrong? Why did the *National Post* fail where Buzzfeed succeeded and what do the two results mean for other publishers?

Part of the reason for the failure is likely to be the nature of the content. Viewers of the Buzzfeed video were waiting to be rewarded by the sight of an exploding watermelon. They were being promised a dramatic, visual moment that could happen at any second. The best that viewers of a cheese-eating contest could hope for was the sight of someone… eating another slice of cheese. Or maybe they'd see a reporter throwing up. Neither of those were things they'd want to stick around for. HBO made a similar mistake when it used Facebook Live to announce the date of the season seven premiere of Game of Thrones. The channel placed the date in a block of ice and invited people to melt it by typing the word "fire" into the comments. Altogether HBO managed to achieve around 100,000 concurrent views… and thousands of complaints about the breakdown in the feed and the sheer dullness of watching ice melt.

It wasn't just the content though. The *Post* also has a different audience. Buzzfeed doesn't release demographic data but it's safe to say that its market is mostly young and the event fit the website's audience closely. The *National Post* is a newspaper. The average age of its readers is 44. About a quarter are aged over 50. They're more likely to see an eating contest as an example of bad parenting than a fun thing to do on a Saturday afternoon.

The *National Post* tried to copy a successful live video failure. It failed, and it failed because it didn't copy the most successful element of that formula, and because it didn't match the content to its audience.

The event should have been an example of successful live video content. Instead, it became a warning against copying a format that worked for one publisher without understanding why it worked or making it match the brand's audience.

The British Museum Goes Global... Live

It was the British who started it. Back in May 2015, as Twitter was killing Meerkat and Periscope was just starting to become known, the venerable old British Museum saw an opportunity. Using TV historian Dan Snow as a host, the museum took viewers around the world on a live tour of its new exhibition, "Defining Beauty: The Body in Ancient Greek Art." For half an hour, Dan Snow showed off works in marble, terracotta and bronze, and explained their importance. At the end of the tour, he took questions through Twitter and Periscope. The video remained visible on Periscope for 24 hours after the tour, and was then moved to Facebook and YouTube.

The broadcast took a little effort but not much. The museum explained that the video was shot on a smartphone customized with a universal wide-angle lens that clipped onto the phone. The phone was placed on a handheld Lanparte gimble to smooth out camera movements. To capture audio, the museum used a Sennheiser wireless lavalier mic with the iRig XLR to minijack adapter. For the Q&A conversation that came at the end, they used a boom mic.

That might all sound very technical but it's all pretty simple and inexpensive. Most of it you can pick up in a local electronics shop. On YouTube, the video has generated over 4,000 views, which might sound disappointing but shorter visions of the tour have generated nearly 60,000 views.

It certainly looked impressive to the Metropolitan Museum which has copied the idea. In April 2016, New York's premiere art museum broadcast live on Facebook from its "Pergamon and the Hellenistic Kingdoms of the Ancient World" exhibition. Two curators took viewers through the show's 264 artworks, a third borrowed from the Pergamon Museum in Berlin. The video on Facebook has been viewed 56,000 times and generated 666 comments from around the world.

Each of those videos had a clear and simple goal: to bring visitors into the exhibition. They took some effort, some organization and some planning but they were both highly useful marketing tools.

Clearly, it's a strategy that can be copied by any artist or gallery owner. But you can expand the principle to include anything that people would want to see. Realtors could do the same thing during an open house. Restaurant owners could take customers on a tour of their dining room after a refurbishment (then take them on a behind-the-scenes tour of the kitchen once the restaurant opens). A retail store could give shoppers a tour of the aisles the evening before a grand sale.

The British Museum might have been showing off some old art, but it also showed an effective way to use the latest technology.

Doritos Plays Russian Roulette Live

Doritos has many of the features that have made Buzzfeed's live videos such a success. The market is primarily young, accustomed to using social media and prepared to view the kind of bizarre live videos that are most prone to going viral.

Those assets haven't been lost on the brand's advertising team. In April 2015, the company took live video's interaction to a whole new level.

Doritos has a product called Roulette. Each bag of traditional nacho cheese chips contains a small number of very spicy chips. The company used that idea to aim at a young, male demographic by creating a social media-based game. Initially the game was played on Twitter. A user would tag three friends with the #DoritosRoulette hashtag. The friends are entered into the contest as a team and winning team names were picked at random on the now-defunct Vine app. That was simple enough but Periscope allowed the company to take things a little further.

Viewers were able to watch a spinning roulette wheel and win prizes based on where the wheel stopped.

Like Buzzfeed's watermelon video, there was a punishment for clicking away: viewers would miss the opportunity to win a prize. Here though, the brand was able to physically reward viewers by handing out valuable prizes in return for watching. When you're a multi-million dollar brand, you can buy views and shares with live video.

Since that early experiment, Doritos has been back for more. Five months after playing roulette live on Periscope, the company promoted its Collisions product, a mixed bag of guacamole and habanero flavored chips, by smashing things up live. For twelve hours, the brand fired objects out of cannons so that they collided in mid-air and broadcast the collisions on Periscope. Marbles met porcelain plates, pies met baseballs, and rubber chickens met bowling balls. Viewers were able to vote on Twitter for the objects they'd like to see smashed together.

Doritos prepared for the event by informing the press and making announcements on social media. When the broadcast ended, slow-motion videos of the best collisions were posted on Twitter, Facebook and YouTube, extending the effectiveness of the event… and showing other brands one way to combine a prepared event with audience interaction.

Benefit Cosmetics Becomes A Broadcast Company

To really understand the power that live video has to change marketing, you don't have to look any further than Benefit Cosmetics. Videos about make-up are nothing new. They're among the most popular topics on YouTube and have made an

Internet star of many an attractive young woman. But Benefit Cosmetics goes further.

Each week the company broadcasts a live make-up workshop on Facebook. That doesn't sound like a big difference. After all, those videos are also available to be seen after the broadcast. But they have a huge effect.

Being able to watch the videos live every week makes the experience much more intense. This isn't just a video watched on a screen. Nor is it a recorded version of the kind of cosmetics trial that women can usually receive in their local drugstore. It's a date with a couple of girlfriends. The presenters aren't unattainable models. They're young women who look, talk and act like the brand's customers. The comments are filled with questions about make-up but also about the wine the girls are drinking. It's not an ad and it's more than a workshop. It's fun with friends. A broadcast typically gets close to 20,000 views.

Benefit Cosmetics has clearly hit on a format that works for its product and for its market. But it's done even more than that. It's also turned itself into an entertainment channel. The company might be in the business of designing cosmetics but it's also now in the business of creating video content in exactly the same way as a television channel. Instead of putting an ad inside a show created by MTV or some other television company, Benefit Cosmetics is using Facebook's platform to put its own show directly in front of its customers and fill it with the content it wants. It's a huge change.

AirBnB Stays At Someone's Else Live Home

AirBnB has also been looking for ways to combine entertainment with its home-sharing platform. In November 2016, the company organized AirBnB Open, "a community-powered festival of travel and hospitality that celebrates a city and its neighborhoods." The aim of the event was to position the company's service not as a product that people buy but as part of an experience that they get to enjoy. The company took over much of downtown LA and used many of the classic theaters on Broadway for talks, shows and performances.

But AirBnB also hijacked someone else's event. The company worked with Disney to live stream the premiere of *The Jungle Book*. AirBnB built a treehouse on the red carpet, interviewed stars and broadcast the event on Facebook. Jonathan Mildenhall, AirBnB's chief marketing officer described engagement as high and said that comments were "incredibly positive." He also said that the company would continue to use live video as part of its goal to become an "experiential brand."

What AirBnB did at *The Jungle Book* premiere was remarkably simple. Instead of creating original content, as Benefit Cosmetics did, it copied wholesale the kind of content that channels like E! might produce and used Facebook's technology to put it in front of an audience. It's little different to sponsorship of a live sports game and it's just as easy for any brand to emulate. There's no reason why a local company couldn't sponsor a local college game, buy the rights to broadcast it on Facebook or Periscope and put their company name in front of their market. They could interview the players and invite the audience to ask their own questions.

AirBnB has shown that you don't have to come up with original live content to benefit from live video. You can just use the content that other people are creating and use live video to send it straight to your own audience.

Conclusion

The evolution of media has taken us from static print ads through the interruption marketing of radio and television commercials to live, interactive broadcasts that audiences choose not just to watch but to participate in. For brands that can create the content, we're at a quantum leap in engagement, in loyalty and in messaging.

The experiences that live video promises are more immediate, more urgent and more interactive than any other form of mass media. It's the difference between building a platform out of plywood and building it out of steel. It's the difference between building it yourself and inviting your friends to come and help build it with you.

Brands have noticed the opportunity. They're already experimenting with content forms, and are setting standards that other brands have to meet. Some of those experiments are coming up short. Others are producing surprising amounts of engagement and reach. As Facebook, Twitter, Instagram and eventually perhaps Snapchat and other platforms continue to add features and enhance their apps, we're likely to see even more experimentation and the further of development of what could well be the most exciting development in content marketing since the first days of blogging.

For businesses, live videos are quickly becoming a perfect channel for transmitting content that can't be delivered any other way with the same effect. They can take audiences behind the scene of a business, cross-market through interviews and conversations, build unique relationships with customers and new leads, and spread around the web with an instant, unmissable appeal.

Live video can't do everything, and it won't replace recorded video, imagery or text content. But it does offer a way to reach audiences that hasn't been seen before.

Live video is here and it's growing. It's time to start using it—and using it right. So fire up your mobile device, launch an app and share your content with the world! They are waiting for your brilliance.

What About Apps and Gear?

In order to keep this short book relevant regardless of software, apps and gear, I've kept the focus on the essentials of live video. It hasn't allowed me the space to discuss storytelling apps (which I consider an important niche within the Live Video Revolution), such as Snapchat, Instagram Stories, Facebook Stories and WhatApp Status.

However, that doesn't mean I've left you in the dark where these things are concerned.

To learn about the latest apps, the newest features, the tools currently available and recommended gear for broadcasting, join The Live Video Academy.

www.Academy.Live

Here you'll discover regular trainings from industry experts, updates and news, reviews of products and services, and more!

About the Author

Joel Comm is *New York Times* bestselling author, professional keynote speaker, social media marketing strategist, live video expert, technologist, brand influencer and futurist. With over two decades of experience harnessing the power of the web, publishing, social media and mobile applications to expand reach and engage in active relationship marketing, Joel is a sought-after public speaker who leaves his audiences inspired, entertained, and armed with strategic tools to create highly effective new media campaigns.

Morgan James
Speakers Group

We connect Morgan James published
authors with live and online events
and audiences who will benefit
from their expertise.